MW00559788

MEL BAY'S DELUXE

# ANTHOLOGY OF FIDDLE STYLES

### by DAVID REINER

## CD Contents

| | | | |
|---|---|---|
| 1 Bile 'Em Cabbage Down [1:01] | 17 Soldiers Joy [1:35] | 32 Finn Jenta Waltz [:45] |
| 2 Mississippi Sawyer [:42] | 18 Old Joe Clark [1:09] | 33 Blues for Cindy [:34] |
| 3 Goin' Up the River [:47] | 19 Ukrainian Breakdown [1:08] | 34 Blues In A [:27] |
| 4 Shortnin' Bread [:40] | 20 Back Up and Push [:35] | 35 La Cassine Special [:52] |
| 5 Scotland the Brave [1:31] | 21 Midnight Waltz [1:24] | 36 Beaumont Rag [1:25] |
| 6 Cucumber Waltz [1:22] | 22 Wabash Cannonball [1:03] | 37 Dusty Miller [1:01] |
| 7 Beer Belly Polka [:49] | 23 Coleraine [:38] | 38 Hard Cider [:56] |
| 8 Intros to Fiddle Tunes [:21] | 24 Kesh Jig [1:07] | 39 Swanee River [1:21] |
| 9 Flop-Eared Mule Schottisch [1:05] | 25 Swallowtail Jig [:39] | 40 Cable [:47] |
| 10 Endings for Fiddle Tunes [1:28] | 26 Drowsy Maggie [:46] | 41 Golden Slippers [:47] |
| 11 Fisher's Hornpipe [:47] | 27 Flowers of Edinburgh [:44] | 42 Liberty Two-Step [:49] |
| 12 Home With the Girls in the Morning [1:31] | 28 High Reel [:46] | 43 Ghost [1:27] |
| 13 Lonesome John [:48] | 29 Si Bheag, Si Mhor [1:29] | 44 Tyska Polska [:56] |
| 14 Red River Valley [:48] | 30 Gärdeby Gånglåt [1:35] | 45 Invitation Rag [:48] |
| 15 Bill Cheatham [:46] | 31 Pols [:44] | 46 Hard Cider [:31] |
| 16 Blackberry Blossom [:52] | | |

1 2 3 4 5 6 7 8 9 0

**Visit us on the Web at www.melbay.com — E-mail us at email@melbay.com**

# ACKNOWLEDGEMENTS

A special thanks to Cindy Eid, whose drawings brighten many of the pages in this book, and to Martha Fritz for her drawings of a butterfly and a bouquet of flowers.

To my musical friends, from whom I learned many tunes, thank you all. This includes Pete Anick, Glenn Asch, John Chambers, Mac Robertson, Tracy Schwarz, Bob Werner, and numerous others. Thanks also to the members of Country Caravan and the Pitz Valley Boys.

The Ph.D thesis of Earl Spielman at the University of Wisconsin provided an excellent overview of American fiddling.

Finally, I am grateful to Bob Swan of Pickin' & Grinnin' Workshops (c/o Innovative Arts, 505 Cottage Grove Rd., Madison, WI 53716) for his constant enthusiasm and hard work which make the workshops possible.

Dave Reiner
c/o Mel Bay Publications
Pacific, Mo. 63069

## Dedicated to Cindy Eid

Cover Photo by Paul Kaarakka

A Cassette Tape of this book is available

# TABLE OF CONTENTS

                                                                    Page
Old-Timey Fiddling.............................................. 7
    Hoedowns and Reels ...................................... 8
    Dance Tunes ............................................15
    Modal Tunes ............................................27
    An Old-Timey Song .....................................29

Bluegrass Fiddling .............................................30

Irish Fiddling .................................................47

Scandinavian Fiddling .........................................56

Blues Fiddling .................................................59

Cajun Fiddling .................................................62

Texas Style and Western Swing Fiddling .........................64

Swing and Jazz Fiddling........................................68

Twin (Harmony) Fiddling........................................76

Bowing .........................................................13

Chords on the Fiddle ...........................................33

Chord Progressions..............................................44

Discography.....................................................85

Improvisation ..................................................74

Kickoffs and Endings for Fiddle Tunes .........................21, 24

## Alphabetical Listing of Tunes

Page

Back Up and Push . . . . . . . . . . . . . . . . . . . . . . . . . . . . . . . . . . . . . . . . . . . . . . . . . . . . . 41
Beaumont Rag . . . . . . . . . . . . . . . . . . . . . . . . . . . . . . . . . . . . . . . . . . . . . . . . . . . . . . . . . 65
Beer Belly Polka . . . . . . . . . . . . . . . . . . . . . . . . . . . . . . . . . . . . . . . . . . . . . . . . . . . . . . . 20
Bile 'Em Cabbage Down . . . . . . . . . . . . . . . . . . . . . . . . . . . . . . . . . . . . . . . . . . . . . 8
Bill Cheatham . . . . . . . . . . . . . . . . . . . . . . . . . . . . . . . . . . . . . . . . . . . . . . . . . . . . . . . . . 31
Blackberry Blossom . . . . . . . . . . . . . . . . . . . . . . . . . . . . . . . . . . . . . . . . . . . . . . . . . . . 32
Blues for Cindy . . . . . . . . . . . . . . . . . . . . . . . . . . . . . . . . . . . . . . . . . . . . . . . . . . . . . . . . 60
Blues In A . . . . . . . . . . . . . . . . . . . . . . . . . . . . . . . . . . . . . . . . . . . . . . . . . . . . . . . . . . . . . 61
Cable . . . . . . . . . . . . . . . . . . . . . . . . . . . . . . . . . . . . . . . . . . . . . . . . . . . . . . . . . . . . . . . . . 72
Coleraine . . . . . . . . . . . . . . . . . . . . . . . . . . . . . . . . . . . . . . . . . . . . . . . . . . . . . . . . . . . . . . 48
Cucumber Waltz . . . . . . . . . . . . . . . . . . . . . . . . . . . . . . . . . . . . . . . . . . . . . . . . . . . . . . . 18
Drowsy Maggie . . . . . . . . . . . . . . . . . . . . . . . . . . . . . . . . . . . . . . . . . . . . . . . . . . . . . . . . 51
Dusty Miller . . . . . . . . . . . . . . . . . . . . . . . . . . . . . . . . . . . . . . . . . . . . . . . . . . . . . . . . . . . 66
Finn Jenta Waltz . . . . . . . . . . . . . . . . . . . . . . . . . . . . . . . . . . . . . . . . . . . . . . . . . . . . . . 58
Fisher's Hornpipe . . . . . . . . . . . . . . . . . . . . . . . . . . . . . . . . . . . . . . . . . . . . . . . . . . . . . 26
Flop-Eared Mule Schottisch . . . . . . . . . . . . . . . . . . . . . . . . . . . . . . . . . . . . . . . . . . 22
Flowers of Edinburgh . . . . . . . . . . . . . . . . . . . . . . . . . . . . . . . . . . . . . . . . . . . . . . . . . 52
Gärdeby Gånglåt . . . . . . . . . . . . . . . . . . . . . . . . . . . . . . . . . . . . . . . . . . . . . . . . . . . . . . 57
Ghost . . . . . . . . . . . . . . . . . . . . . . . . . . . . . . . . . . . . . . . . . . . . . . . . . . . . . . . . . . . . . . . . . 80
Goin' Up the River . . . . . . . . . . . . . . . . . . . . . . . . . . . . . . . . . . . . . . . . . . . . . . . . . . . . 11
Golden Slippers . . . . . . . . . . . . . . . . . . . . . . . . . . . . . . . . . . . . . . . . . . . . . . . . . . . . . . . 77
Hard Cider . . . . . . . . . . . . . . . . . . . . . . . . . . . . . . . . . . . . . . . . . . . . . . . . . . . 69, 84
High Reel . . . . . . . . . . . . . . . . . . . . . . . . . . . . . . . . . . . . . . . . . . . . . . . . . . . . . . . . . . . . . 54
Home With the Girls in the Morning . . . . . . . . . . . . . . . . . . . . . . . . . . . . . . . . . 27
Invitation Rag . . . . . . . . . . . . . . . . . . . . . . . . . . . . . . . . . . . . . . . . . . . . . . . . . . . . . . . . 83
Kesh Jig . . . . . . . . . . . . . . . . . . . . . . . . . . . . . . . . . . . . . . . . . . . . . . . . . . . . . . . . . . . . . . 49
La Cassine Special . . . . . . . . . . . . . . . . . . . . . . . . . . . . . . . . . . . . . . . . . . . . . . . . . . . 63
Liberty Two-Step . . . . . . . . . . . . . . . . . . . . . . . . . . . . . . . . . . . . . . . . . . . . . . . . . . . . . 78
Lonesome John . . . . . . . . . . . . . . . . . . . . . . . . . . . . . . . . . . . . . . . . . . . . . . . . . . . . . . . . 28
Midnight Waltz . . . . . . . . . . . . . . . . . . . . . . . . . . . . . . . . . . . . . . . . . . . . . . . . . . . . . . . . 42
**Mississippi Sawyer** . . . . . . . . . . . . . . . . . . . . . . . . . . . . . . . . . . . . . . . . . . . . . . . . . **10**

Old Joe Clark . . . . . . . . . . . . . . . . . . . . . . . . . . . . . . . . . . . . . . . . . . . . . . . . . . . . . . . . . 38
Pols . . . . . . . . . . . . . . . . . . . . . . . . . . . . . . . . . . . . . . . . . . . . . . . . . . . . . . . . . . . . . . . . . . . 58
Red River Valley . . . . . . . . . . . . . . . . . . . . . . . . . . . . . . . . . . . . . . . . . . . . . . . . . . . . . . 29
Scotland the Brave . . . . . . . . . . . . . . . . . . . . . . . . . . . . . . . . . . . . . . . . . . . . . . . . . . . . 16
Shortnin' Bread . . . . . . . . . . . . . . . . . . . . . . . . . . . . . . . . . . . . . . . . . . . . . . . . . . . . . . . 12
Si Bheag, Si Mhor . . . . . . . . . . . . . . . . . . . . . . . . . . . . . . . . . . . . . . . . . . . . . . . . . . . . 55
Soldier's Joy . . . . . . . . . . . . . . . . . . . . . . . . . . . . . . . . . . . . . . . . . . . . . . . . . . . . . . . . . . 37
Swallowtail Jig . . . . . . . . . . . . . . . . . . . . . . . . . . . . . . . . . . . . . . . . . . . . . . . . . . . . . . . . 50
Swanee River . . . . . . . . . . . . . . . . . . . . . . . . . . . . . . . . . . . . . . . . . . . . . . . . . . . . . . . . . 71
Tyska Polska . . . . . . . . . . . . . . . . . . . . . . . . . . . . . . . . . . . . . . . . . . . . . . . . . . . . . . . . . . 82
Ukrainian Breakdown . . . . . . . . . . . . . . . . . . . . . . . . . . . . . . . . . . . . . . . . . . . . . . . . . 40
Wabash Cannonball . . . . . . . . . . . . . . . . . . . . . . . . . . . . . . . . . . . . . . . . . . . . . . . . . . . 46

# INTRODUCTION

This book owes its existence, in part, to the Pickin' & Grinnin' Workshops that have been held for the last four or five years, mainly in Wisconsin. As fiddle instructor at the workshops, I encountered a wide variety of fiddlers, ranging from absolute beginners to classical violinists interested in finding out just what fiddling was all about. Most of the transcriptions in this book are of tunes I've taught at these weekend workshops.

Recently, interest has been growing in the art of fiddling. The fact is, whether you're playing in your own living room, or in a band with your friends, fiddling is a lot of fun. What is confusing at times is the multiplicity of styles which the aspiring fiddler is confronted with. By presenting a selection of tunes from a number of American fiddling traditions, I hope to give you a better feeling for the differences among them.

Later, of course, you may wish to concentrate on just one style, but I think you'll be the richer for having tried the others. You'll be better prepared to jam along on new tunes, and may find yourself developing a flexible, composite **style**.

I've tried to indicate the exact bowings, double notes, and tempos I use in playing these tunes. Slides are represented by arrows: for example, an up-arrow ($\nearrow$) before a C# means to slide quickly from a C to the C#. The special notation is explained in the bowing section. Other than these differences, I've used standard musical notation throughout.

Now, some people say that you really can't learn a fiddle tune from paper. To an **extent** they're right, and this is where the discography comes in. It is important to listen to as much fiddling as you can. Not only will this help you to train your ear, as you try to pick up tunes from the records, but you'll also become familiar with the sound and "feel" of fiddling. Then it will be easier to reproduce in your own playing.

I'm sure you'll enjoy playing with other people. The chords are provided for each tune, written above the music, to make it easier for other musicians to play along with you. The fiddle is traditionally backed up by a guitar or piano, but banjos and mandolins are always welcome. (So are basses, dulcimers, autoharps, harmonicas, or what have you. Music is meant to be shared.)

Certain tunes have been written with several versions. Sometimes the versions are increasingly difficult, sometimes just different. You'll note that most fiddle tunes have the common structure of a first (or "A") part, and a second (or "B") part. Each of these should be repeated, so that the order of playing is AABBAABBAABB...until you're tired. Fiddlers often give a four beat introduction to tunes, and end with a catchy ending. (See the section on kickoffs and ending tags.)

If another instrument takes the lead, be subtle in your backup. Mostly that means playing quietly, so as not to clutter up the tune with a lot of notes. Again listening is important.

I think that the sections on bowing, chords, chord progressions, and improvising should prove helpful. You may wish to read them over several times, as they are quite condensed.

While most tunes in this book are primarily for the intermediate or advanced fiddler, there are a number of tunes suitable for beginners. Try the first three versions of Bile 'Em Cabbage Down, Shortnin' Bread, Home With the Girls In the Morning, Red River Valley, Versions I and II of Old Joe Clark, and the first versions of Soldier's Joy and Wabash Cannonball. Practice them slowly at first, until you are sure of the intonation and bowing.

Well, take out your fiddle, rosin the bow, and enjoy the tunes!

David Reiner

# OLD TIMEY FIDDLING

First brought to America by British **settlers,** the fiddle quickly became the dominant instrument in early American community activities. The fiddler, a man of stature in his community, was an indispensible fixture at weddings, dances, barn raisings, and other social gatherings. Particularly at dances, the fiddle was in its element. Hoedowns, reels, waltzes, hornpipes, polkas, and jigs flowed from the instrument, to the delight of the listeners and dancers.

"Old-Timey" is the term generally applied to this style of playing, which is still widespread in the United States. Often, Appalachian modal tunes, old songs played on the fiddle, and listening pieces not suitable for dancing, are also classified as old-timey.

# BILE 'EM CABBAGE DOWN

Here's a fine hoedown that never fails to get people stompin'.
I like to use it to start off a Virginia reel.

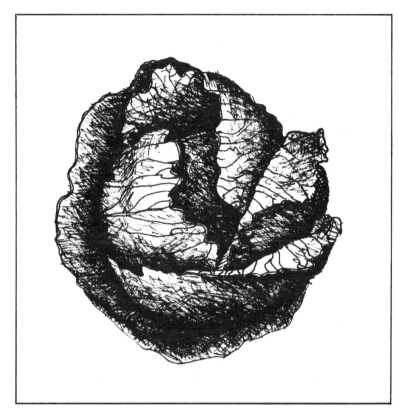

# MISSISSIPPI SAWYER

This is an excellent square dance tune, which was first played, according to tradition, by a sawmill operator in Mississippi--whence the name. Some fiddlers use an A chord instead of the C chord in the second half, but I think the tune is more interesting like this. I have included the guitar part to give your backup guitarist an idea of the appropriate backup style for old-timey and bluegrass fiddling.

10

Man, Woman, and Fire    KATHRYN GERHARDT

# GOIN' UP THE RIVER

This is a cheerful, bouncy tune. In the second measure of the B part, a half-step change (from C# to C) marks the transition from the A chord to the D⁷—a useful trick to know.

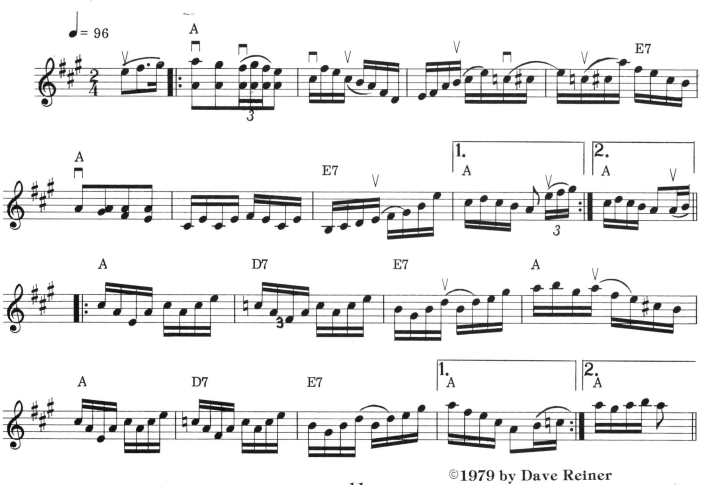

# SHORTNIN' BREAD

Shortnin' Bread is a good tune for beginners. By accenting the off-beat as shown, you can give the tune a real old-time flavor. Try the fourth measure both ways (with a C - natural and a C-sharp) to see which you prefer.

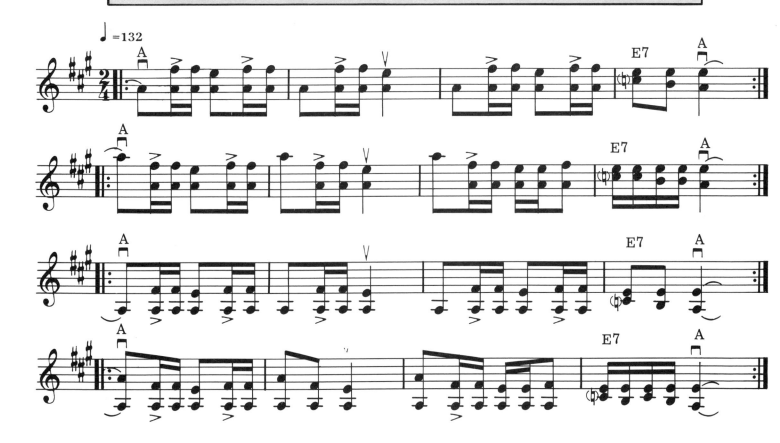

Farm in Snow    BRUCE FRITZ

# BOWING

Much of the feeling of a fiddle tune comes from the way it **is** bowed. The drive of a hoedown and the cheerful lilt of an Irish jig depend, at least in part, on the fiddler's choice of bowing patterns. Even within a given musical tradition, such as bluegrass, each fiddler gradually develops his own style of bowing, which is often quite distinctive and recognizable.

While the tunes in this book all include bowing indications, you should take them more as suggestions than hard-and-fast rules. Feel free to experiment with the bowing for each tune until you are comfortable with it.

I have used the standard notation of ⊓ for a downbow and ⌄ for an upbow. Notes to be slurred together on the same bow are indicated by the symbol ⌢ or ⌣ tying the notes together. Where bowing marks are not written in, bow as in the preceeding measures.

The easiest bowing for a reel, or any other tune in ² ₄ or ³ ₄ time, is the back-and-forth **saw stroke:** ⊓⌄⊓⌄ ⊓⌄⊓⌄ . Most fiddlers use approximately the top third of the bow, attacking each note equally. Another common bowing technique is the **Nashville shuffle,** consisting of a long bow stroke followed by two short ones, repeated over and over: ⊓ ⌄⊓ ⌄ ⊓ ⌄ or ⊓⌢ ⌄⊓ ⌄⌢⊓⌄ . Both the Nashville shuffle and the saw stroke let you begin each measure on a downbow, which emphasizes the beat and helps you to keep track of time.

A technique which emphasizes the beat and also gives a flowing quality to the notes is the **1-3-1-3** division of a measure: ⊓ ⌄⌢ ⊓ ⌄⌢ . See the B part of Fisher's Hornpipe for an example. When the downbow is displaced to the offbeat, this pattern becomes the **Georgia shuffle:** ⌄⌢ ⊓⌄⌢ ⊓⌄⌢ . Here the last upbow in a measure crosses over into the next measure. Although I often use a Nashville shuffle for Soldier's Joy I have written the A part of version III of the tune using the Georgia shuffle. Note how the Nashville shuffle dissolves into the Georgia shuffle in the first measure: ⊓⌢⌄⊓ ⌄⌢⊓⌄ .

**Whichever shuffle is used, fiddlers (especially old-timey fiddlers) often put a strong accent on the offbeat, providing a contrasting rhythm to the beat, and making tunes sound jumpy and more alive.**

To **smooth** out a tune, you may slur more notes on a bow: 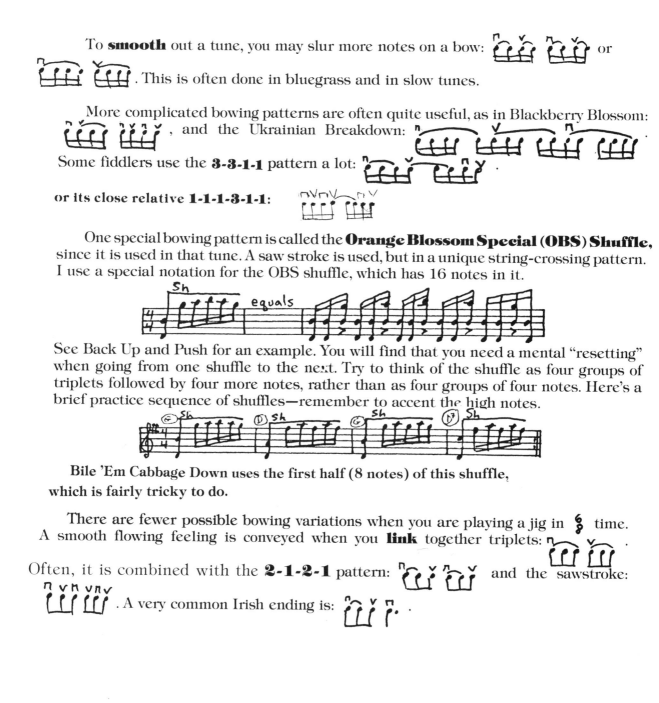 or
. This is often done in bluegrass and in slow tunes.

More complicated bowing patterns are often quite useful, as in Blackberry Blossom:
, and the Ukrainian Breakdown: .
Some fiddlers use the **3-3-1-1** pattern a lot: .

or its close relative **1-1-1-3-1-1**:

One special bowing pattern is called the **Orange Blossom Special (OBS) Shuffle,**
since it is used in that tune. A saw stroke is used, but in a unique string-crossing pattern.
I use a special notation for the OBS shuffle, which has 16 notes in it.

See Back Up and Push for an example. You will find that you need a mental "resetting"
when going from one shuffle to the next. Try to think of the shuffle as four groups of
triplets followed by four more notes, rather than as four groups of four notes. Here's a
brief practice sequence of shuffles—remember to accent the high notes.

**Bile 'Em Cabbage Down** uses the first half (8 notes) of this shuffle,
which is fairly tricky to do.

There are fewer possible bowing variations when you are playing a jig in $\frac{6}{8}$ time.
A smooth flowing feeling is conveyed when you **link** together triplets: .

Often, it is combined with the **2-1-2-1** pattern: and the sawstroke:
. A very common Irish ending is: .

# DANCE TUNES

Playing for dances is enjoyable but challenging. It helps a lot to have done a particular dance yourself, for then you'll have a feeling for the right tempo. Watch the dancers—if they're gasping for breath and making wild gestures in your direction it's probably a good idea to slow down. If there is a caller, watch him for signals to speed up or slow down, or to end the tune.

You may find yourself leading the band. In that case, make sure that the beat is clear, stay close to the melody, and see that the musicians have warning if you're going to switch tunes in the middle. If you are using a sound system, resist the urge to turn it way up.

Glenn Wood, an old-timey and jazz
fiddler from Wisconsin    PETE ANICK

# SCOTLAND THE BRAVE

Scotland the Brave is a march, so you will want a heavy accent on the beat. Some fiddlers tune the G-string down four steps to a low D note, in order to imitate the drone of bagpipes.

# CUCUMBER WALTZ

Fiddling contests often require a hoedown, a waltz, and a third tune of the player's choice, such as a hornpipe, rag, jig, or reel. A slow waltz is indeed a good test of a fiddler's abilities, as it must be expressive and light-hearted at the same time.    Vibrato on the long notes is helpful.

# BEER BELLY POLKA

Play this fine polka in a lively fashion, with plenty of bounce to your bow.

**Intro** ♩ = 144

**Verse 1 & 3**

It ain't so hard to get rid of that lard, A whole lot of oth - er good folk have.   Get
Ain't it a shame to hear women complain, A-bout something we've no con - trol of.___   It

out on the floor with the girl you a - dore, And dance to the beer belly pol - ka.
gets on their nerves___ to see men with curves, danc - ing the beer belly pol - ka.

**Verse 2 & 4**

If you think your bel - ly's too big, Take a drink, dance to the mus - ic.
If you think your wife 'll bop you, Take a drink, don't let her stop you.

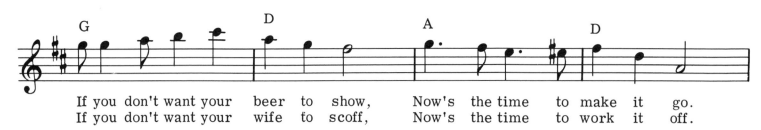

If you don't want your beer to show, Now's the time to make it go.
If you don't want your wife to scoff, Now's the time to work it off.

You'll be as slender as our friend the bartend er   Dancing the beer belly pol - ka.
It's just as nice___ as___ doing ex - er - cis - es   Dancing the beer belly pol - ka.

# KICKOFFS AND ENDINGS FOR FIDDLE TUNES

## INTRODUCTIONS
## (KICKOFFS) TO FIDDLE TUNES

# FLOP-EARED MULE SCHOTTISCH

A schottisch is a hopping dance done by couples or pairs of couples. Flop-Eared Mule is usually played as a reel, but works well in this slower dotted rhythm.

# Endings For Fiddle Tunes

Key of G

Key of C

25

# FISHER'S HORNPIPE

Although hornpipes are often written with straight eighth notes, they are customarily played as ♩♪♪♪ or ♩.♫♩.♫ Note the 1-3-1-3 bowing in the second part.

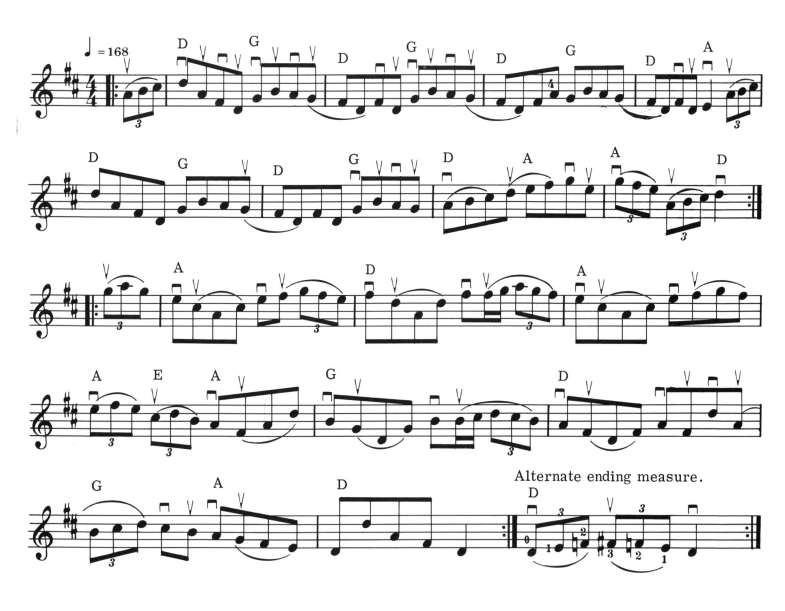

Alternate ending measure.

# MODAL TUNES

# HOME WITH THE GIRLS IN THE MORNING

> Many Appalachian modal tunes are done in Dorian mode, where the scale is
> A, B, C, D, E, F♯, G, A (in the key of A). This gives them a lonely, minor
> sound. In the B part, there is an ear-startling A major chord the second time
> through, which contrasts sharply with the minor modality of the tune.

gradually slowing

# LONESOME JOHN

Lonesome John is another fine modal tune. I've heard several variations on the melody. The rising arrows above and before C-notes indicate slides slightly beyond a C-natural.

# An Old-Timey Song

# RED RIVER VALLEY

A traditional American song, Red River Valley sounds quite nice on the fiddle. Notice how much the double stops in Version II add to the sound. Nearly continuous use of drone strings is referred to as "keeping a full fiddle".

# Bluegrass Fiddling

In the middle 1940's, Bill Monroe assembled a band consisting of fiddle, mandolin, five-string banjo, guitar, and bass. Featuring hard-driving instrumentals and tight harmony vocals, this was the first bluegrass band. I've heard bluegrass called "folk music with overdrive".

A bluegrass fiddler must be able to play lead, rhythm, and backup lines for vocal tunes as well as instrumentals. However, in this section of the book I have concentrated mainly on bluegrass versions of instrumental tunes. Although these are sometimes similar to what an old-timey fiddler would play, they are generally played for a listening audience only.

# BILL CHEATHAM

Bill Cheatham is a lively reel, which should be played cleanly and quickly.

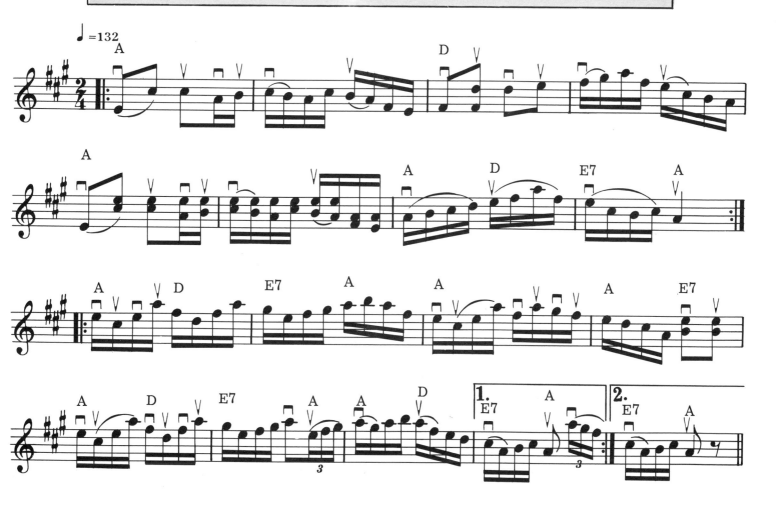

# BLACKBERRY BLOSSOM

The light, airy melody of measures one and two reappears in a slightly changed form three more times in the A section. The B part has a bluesy feel to it, and should be played very smoothly.

# CHORDS ON THE FIDDLE

It is certainly possible to play the fiddle without any knowledge of music theory. However, I recommend that you familiarize yourself with at least the basic ideas of scales, chords, chord progressions, and reading music. This information will help you to:
+ Understand your instrument
+ Use the correct notes when you are playing more than one string
+ Improvise more readily
+ Play accompaniment or harmonies with other musicians
+ Communicate about musical ideas and "licks"
+ Learn new tunes from the growing literature of fiddle music.
Quite a list, right? It doesn't all happen at once, of course, but the basic knowledge is not too complicated. I will assume that you know how to read music, since you've made it this far in the book, and we'll start by talking about scales.

## Major Scales
There are 12 tones within an octave, each tone a half-step higher than the previous one. They are:

A (A♯ or B♭) B C (C♯ or D♭) D (D♯ or E♭) E F (F♯ or G♭) G (G♯ or A♭).
1         2    3 4      5        6      7      8 9     10      11    12

The next tone would be another A, an octave above the first A.
As you can see, a sharp (♯) raises the pitch of a note by a half-step, while a flat (♭) lowers it by a half-step. Certain notes have two names; for example, A♯ and B♭ describe the same note. (This is true for most instruments, but not <u>exactly</u> correct for a violin.) An interval between notes of two half steps (e.g. C to D) is called a whole step.
**A major scale is an eight note sequence, starting on any of the 12 tones, which is characterized by the following intervals between successive tones: whole step, whole step, half step, whole step, whole step, whole step, half step. Here is a D-major scale:**

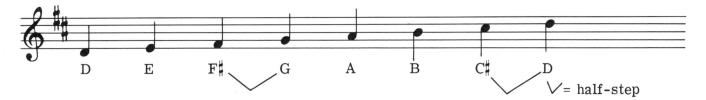

The half-steps are from F♯ to G and from C♯ to D. Two sharps (F♯ and C♯) are required in the key signature to maintain the correct intervals between successive notes. When you play a fiddle tune in the key of D, you are likely to start and end on a D note, and to use only the notes in the D scale (with a few exceptions to be discussed later.) A G♯ would not fit in well since it is not in the scale. Here are major scales in the other common fiddling keys:

Chords

A major chord is composed of the 1st, 3rd, and 5th notes of the corresponding major scale. A G-major chord is thus made up of the notes G, B, and D.

    1   2   3   4   5   6   7   8  G-major chord

From the notes of a G-major chord, we can form a G-major arpeggio:

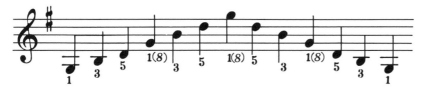

By referring back to the corresponding scale, you can figure out the notes in any major chord. For example, a D-major chord is composed of D, F♯, and A.

A G-minor chord uses the 1st, flatted 3rd, and 5th notes of the G scale, and is made up of the notes G, B♭, and D. A D-minor chord would be D, F, and A.

The following table tells you what the notes are in all common chords:

| Chord | Notes from Scale |
|---|---|
| Major | 1 - 3 - 5 |
| Minor | 1 - flat 3 - 5 |
| 7th | 1 - 3 - 5 - flat 7 |
| 6th | 1 - 3 - 5 - 6 |
| Augmented | 1 - 3 - sharp 5 |
| Diminished | 1 - flat 3 - sharp 4 - 6 ($1\frac{1}{2}$ step intervals) |
| Major 7th | 1 - 3 - 5 - 7 |
| Minor 7th | 1 - flat 3 - 5 - flat 7 |
| 9th | 1 - 3 - 5 - flat 7 - 9 |
| Suspended 7th | 1 - 4 - 5 - flat 7 |

Here are examples in the key of C, using the common chord symbols:

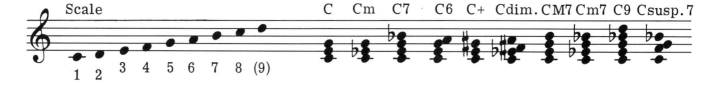

Fortunately, most fiddle tunes require only major (and sometimes 7th) chords!
The rest are given mainly for the sake of completeness. Since you usually play only one or two notes at a time on the fiddle, it is impossible to play complete chords.
This makes life easier, since you need only play part of the chord, letting the other instruments (such as guitar) fill in the rest of the notes. For example, all playable pairs of notes from the G arpeggio can be considered G-major chords:

Some sound more complete, or tighter, than others. Those marked with an asterisk (*) are the most common. They usually include the root (1st note ) and either the 3rd or 5th notes of the G scale.

Playing the 6th (or flatted 7th) note in the scale is often sufficient to suggest a 6th (or 7th) chord.

When you are in the middle of chording accompaniment to a fiddle tune, you don't have time to figure out every chord from the corresponding scale. Fortunately, you don't have to, since relatively few finger positions will give you most chords that you need.

Major Chord Table:

| Finger Positions | | | G-D | D-A | A-E | (Pairs of Strings) |
|---|---|---|---|---|---|---|
| Low - High | | | | | | (How to read table: |
| String String | | | | | | High 2nd finger on the |
| 3 - 1 | * | | C | G | D | D-string (F♯) plus 3rd |
| 1 - low 2 | * | | F | C | G | finger on the A-string |
| 1 - high 2 | * | | D | A | E | (D) gives a D chord.) |
| high 2 - 3 | * | | G | Ⓓ | A | |
| high 2 - 0 (open) | | | G | D | A | (same as high 2 - 3) |
| high 3 - 1 | | | A | E | B | |
| 0 - 0 | m | | G | D | A | |
| low 1 - low 1 | m | | G♯(A♭) | D♯(E♭) | A♯(B♭) | |
| 1 - 1 | m,* | | A | E | B | (same as high 3 - 1) |
| low 2 - low 2 | m | | A♯(B♭) | F | C | |
| high 2 - high 2 | m | | B | F♯(G♭) | C♯(D♭) | |
| 3 - 3 | m | | C | G | D | (same as 3 - 1) |
| high 2 - 1 | m | | E | B | F♯(G♭) | |
| 0 - low 1 | | | D♯(E♭) | A♯(B♭) | F | |
| 3 - low 2 | m | | F | C | G | (same as 1 - low 2) |
| 4 - high 2 | | | D | A | E | (same as 1 - high 2) |

The most common chords in the above table are marked with an asterisk (*). If you know these, you will be able to chord along with almost any fiddle tune. The chords marked with an 'm' can also be used as minor chords.

Note that the same chord can often be played in many different positions. It is best to pick the version of the chord which is convenient to reach from the previous chord, and which sounds good with the melody at that point. Often this means that you will play a series of chords on one pair of adjacent strings, such as D-A, rather than skipping around.

Seventh chords feel slightly strained on the fiddle. The best 7th chords are those with a higher finger crossing over a lower one to play on a lower string. This position is always the 3rd and flatted 7th notes of the scale, which are enough to sound like a 7th chord.

Seventh Chord Table:

| Finger Positions | | G-D | D-A | A-E | (Pairs of Strings) |
|---|---|---|---|---|---|
| Low  -  High String    String | | | | | |
| low 1 - 0 (open) | | Bb7(A#7) | F7 | C7 | |
| 1 - low 1 | | F7 | C7 | G7 | (2nd finger used to |
| low 2 - 1 | * | C7 | G7 | D7 | get the 1 position) |
| high 2 - low 2 | * | G7 | D7 | A7 | (3rd finger used to |
| 3 - high 2 | * | D7 | A7 | E7 | get the high 2 pos.) |
| low 4 - 3 | | A7 | E7 | B7 | |

The most common chords are again marked with an asterisk (*).
(Each finger position in the table actually gives you two different 7th chords. A low
2nd finger on the G-string (Bb) and a 1st finger on the D-string (E) give you a C7 chord,
but if the 2nd finger is regarded as an A#, then the chord can also be regarded as an
F#7 chord. Go up three full steps from the chord listed in the table to find the alternate
name (C7 + three full steps = F#7). The chords are usually used the way they are listed
in the table, however.)

Chording accompaniment is done with short upbow strokes on the offbeat. I find it
helpful to stomp my foot on the beat, while chording on the offbeat. Alternatively, you
may hold the notes out, or use a shuffle rhythm. Be careful with the shuffle, as it tends
to clutter up the tune when another instrument is playing melody.
Here are the three possibilities written out:

If other instruments such as guitar and bass are carrying the rhythm, you may
wish to use a more complicated accompaniment if it seems to fit in well.
See the section on improvising for some hints.

# SOLDIER'S JOY

Probably every American fiddler knows Soldier's Joy. For a variation, I sometimes play version II in D-minor (with F-natural, C-natural, and B-natural) and call it Soldier's Sorrow. Then the chords are mostly Dm and C.

# OLD JOE CLARK

An old-time fiddler might use Version II, perhaps adding Nashville shuffle bowing ( ♪♪♪♪ instead of ♪♪♪ ) in the A part. The bluegrass approach in Version III is to weave notes around the melody to produce a continuous flow. In either style, Old Joe Clark is an exciting tune with lots of drive.

# UKRAINIAN BREAKDOWN

I would classify this tune as "newgrass", meaning bluegrass influenced by various other styles including rock and jazz. The second break for the A part is a strange one, but fun to play.

(first half only)

Harmonic

# BACK UP AND PUSH

Here's a good example of bluegrass double-stopping, with a B part full of double shuffles as an added attraction. This type of shuffle can also be called the OBS (Orange Blossom Special) shuffle or the "hokum" shuffle. See the bowing section for more information.

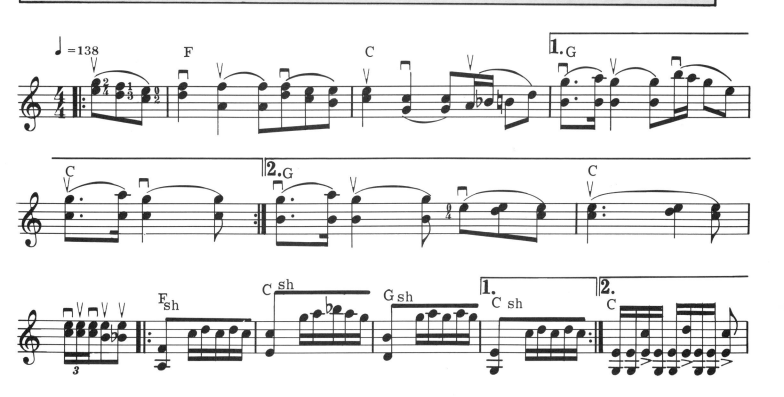

# MIDNIGHT WALTZ

Midnight is a very beautiful bluegrass waltz, relaxed in some spots, with bursts of energy in others. To get the last chord, either rock the bow, or press down hard enough to play three strings at once.

# CHORD PROGRESSIONS

Each note in a major scale may be used as the root (first) note of a new chord. These new chords are customarily denoted by Roman numerals indicating their place in the original major scale. For example, in the key of G we have this sequence of notes and associated chords:

| G | A | B | C | D | E | (F) | F# |
|---|---|---|---|---|---|-----|-----|
| I | II | III | IV | V | VI | (flat VII) | VII |

We say that a D-major chord is the V chord in the key of G.

Many fiddle tunes use a I-IV-V-I chord progression (sequence of chords), or some variant thereof. In the key of G, this would be G-C-D-G. Look at the chords of Wabash Cannonball (WC) for an example. If you played the tune in a different key, the chord progression would be the same, but the chords themselves would be different.

| Key | I | - | IV | - | V | - | I |
|-----|---|---|-----|---|---|---|---|
| C | C | | F | | G | | C |
| G | G | | C | | D | | G |
| D | D | | G | | A | | D |
| A | A | | D | | E | | A |

To play WC in the key of G, a fiddler might use these chords (from the fingering chart in the section on chords):

The same finger positions, moved up by a string, would serve for chording accompaniment in the key of D (see above right). Move them to the bottom strings, and the progression would be in the key of C.

Another common progression, which occurs in Old Joe Clark, is I-VII-I-VII-I. (Here, "VII" stands for the dominant, or flat VII chord, as is customary. Since OJC is in A, the VII chord is a G chord.) Progressions can become quite complicated, (see Hard Cider and Cucumber **Waltz**), but most fiddle tunes are based on fairly simple progressions.

Table of Some Common Progressions

| Type | Progression | In the Key of G |
|------|-------------|-----------------|
| Folk, Old-Time | I-IV-V-I | G-C-D-G |
| Hoedown | I-V-I | G-D-G |
| Ragtime | I-VI$^7$-II$^7$-V$^7$-I | G-E$^7$-A$^7$-D$^7$-G |
| Country | I-IV-I-V-I-IV-I-V$^7$-I | G-C-G-D-G-C-G-D$^7$-G |
| Blues | I-I$^7$-IV-I-V-IV-I | GGGG$^7$CCGGDCGG (12-bar blues) |
| Modal | I-VII-I | G-F-G |

(Lower case Roman numerals, should you ever run into them, stand for minor chords.) Take some time to chord through these progressions, using chords from the section on chording, in order to train your ear to recognize them. A very common ending tag, by the way, is I-V$^7$-I. (See the section on ending tags for fiddle tunes.)

44

If you are playing with a guitarist, it is very helpful to watch his fingers at first. After a short while, you will recognize the most common chords on the guitar, and be able to pick out the progressions that way. The more you play, and especially the more you **listen,** the easier it will be to hear certain recurring progressions such as I-IV, V-I, and I-VII-I. When you can hear the chord changes occurring, and know simple chords reasonably well on the fiddle, you will be able to chord along with fiddle tunes or songs that you have never heard before.

Seventh chords create tension, which can be resolved by progressing to the chord five steps below. That is, a V⁷ chord is often followed by a return to the I chord. In the key of G, it is common to interpose a D⁷ chord between a D and a G, to create the modified progression G-C-D-D⁷-G (I-IV-V-V⁷-I). It is easy to hear the 7th being added (remember a 7th chord is composed of 1-3-5-flat 7, which is a major chord (1-3-5) plus one added note (flat 7)), and that almost inevitably signals the coming chord change. In a similar fashion, a I⁷ chord often occurs between a I chord and a IV chord. This would be G-G⁷-C in the key of G. Incidentally, a convenient way to resolve the 7th chords from the 7th chord table on **page 36** is to "swap" your fingers. For example, G⁷ to C would be:

When the progression goes down five steps several times in succession, this is known as a "circle of fifths", common in ragtime, swing, and sometimes bluegrass music. Look at the Beer Belly Polka. (B-Em-A-D) = (VI-iim-V-I).

I haven't really said **why** a certain chord progression fits with a given tune. Basically it comes down to this: the important melody notes nearly always fall on the 1, 3, or 5 notes from the corresponding chord. When the melody line in WC goes from a G note to an E note at the end of the second measure, this signals a chord change, since there is no E in a G chord. In theory, several choices are possible for the new chord. It could be a G⁶, which **does** contain an E, or perhaps an E-major (unlikely, since that would include a G#, which clashes with the preceeding G note), or an E-minor (conceivable, but WC does not sound like a minor tune), or a C.

In fact, the new chord is almost guaranteed to be a C, the second chord in the I-IV-V-I progression. A C **sounds** right, and any other chord sounds wrong in the context of the tune.

Once you know that a C chord fits in, you can add a G note (open G string) or a C note (third finger on the G string) to the E melody note to fill out the C chord. This is known as "double-stopping", or using a "drone" string, to create your own harmony notes. The open string drone is easier, but the third finger sounds better since it produces a tighter chord. Try both of them to hear the difference:

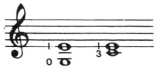

Since E, A, D, and G notes (the open strings) appear often in the I, IV, and V chords of the common fiddling keys (C, G, D, and A), the open string above or below the melody note will often work well **as a** drone string. This is not true of strange keys such as E♭, which probably explains why fiddlers prefer the keys that they do.

# WABASH CANNONBALL

You've probably heard this song before. Although based on a simple I–IV–V–I progression, it is a dynamic melody which lends itself easily to improvisation.

# IRISH FIDDLING

Irish immigrants to the United States asserted their iden-
tity in the music they brought with them. The traditional dance
music of rural Ireland thrived in big cities such as New York
and Chicago, reaching its height of popularity in the 1920's.
Together with flute & penny whistle players, bagpipers, and
an occasional bodhran (Irish drum) player, Irish-American
musicians fiddled at weddings, dances, and bars.

# COLERAINE

Irish jigs in minor keys have a special charm to them, and **Coleraine** is one of the best.  There are no strong accents in the tune--keep it moving lightly along.

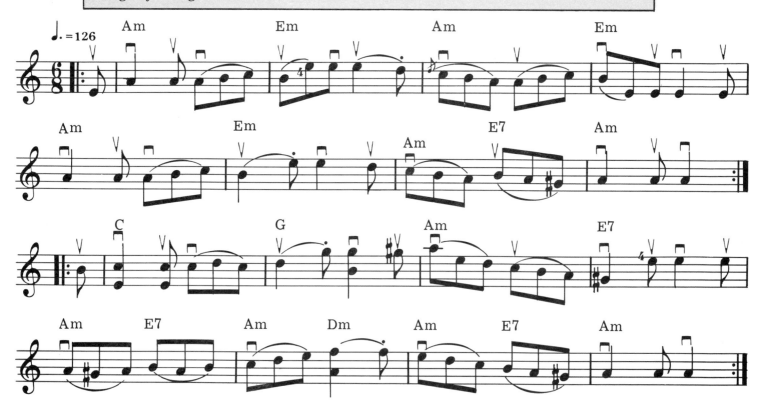

# KESH JIG

Version II of the Kesh Jig is ornamented in typically Irish fashion.
Don't use all of the turns and added notes every time you play the tune,
but throw them in occasionally for variety.

49

# SWALLOWTAIL JIG

This jig has a strong accent on the beat, especially in the A part. Try playing the A part of Swallowtail up an octave.

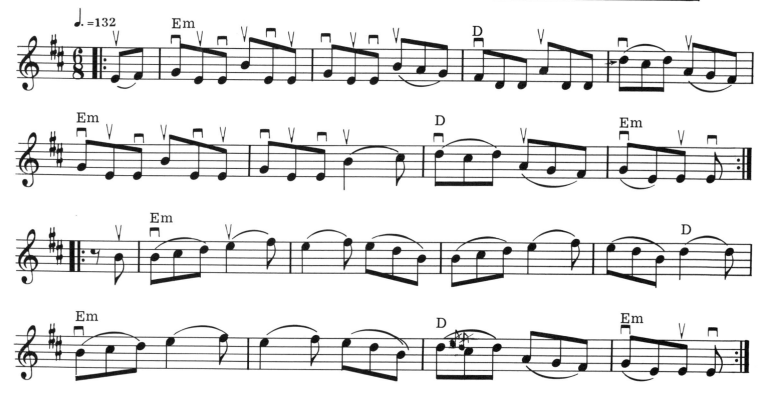

Arr. © 1978 by D. Reiner and J. Chambers. Used by permission.

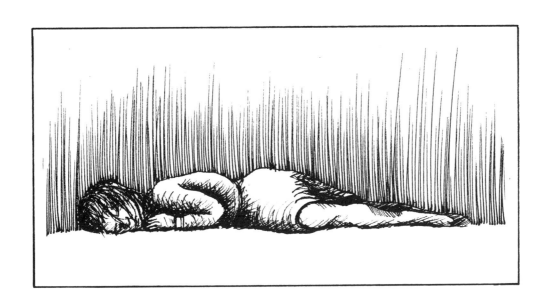

# DROWSY MAGGIE

To imitate the sound of a pennywhistle or bagpipe player, cut the first note short in each pair of eighth notes in the A part. ♪ ♪♪♪♪♪ is then played more like ♪ ♪♪·♪♪♪·

# FLOWERS OF EDINBURGH

This Irish reel has a beautiful melody, which sounds great when several instruments (fiddle, mandolin, and **accordion** for example) play in unison. In general, Irish musicians do not use harmony. They all play the melody line, using complex arrangements where instruments are added in one or two at a time. Often several tunes are combined into a medley.

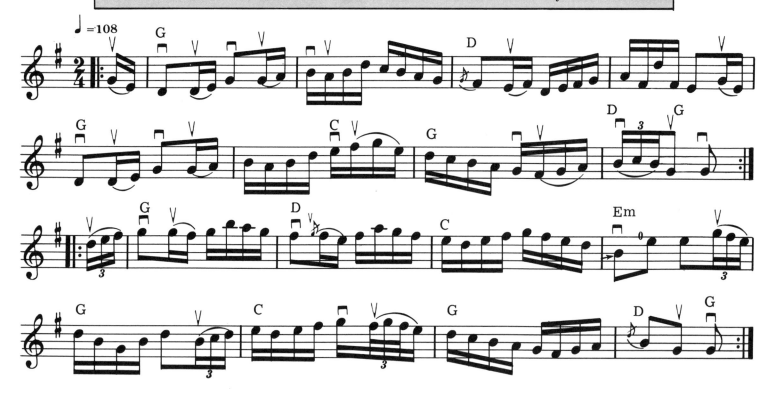

Wood Cabin    DON KERKHOF

# HIGH REEL

This is a typical Irish reel, including triple bounce bowing, triplets, and phrasing which imitates a whistle. The A and B parts are quite similar, and it will be easier to memorize the tune if you are aware of its structure.

# SI BHEAG, SI MHOR

The literal meaning of the title (in Gaelic) is "So Big, So Little". It has been suggested that "Si" is derived from the **medieval** Irish "Siod", meaning "Fairy Hill" or "Mound", so the title might also be translated as "Big Hill, Little Hill". This slow air should be played in an unhurried fashion, with vibrato.

Cows in Field    DON KERKHOF

# SCANDINAVIAN FIDDLING

Norwegian and Swedish immigrants to America brought with them the strong fiddling traditions of the Scandinavian countries. Although Scandinavian fiddlers received the vigorous support of their villages back home, they have tended through the years to become more isolated in this country, now playing mostly at house parties.

Scandinavian fiddlers often play in harmony, and sometimes use eight- or nine-string, heavily-ornamented, **Hardanger** fiddles. These are tuned like a regular violin (except for the G string which is usually tuned up a step to "A"),but have four or five drone strings running under the fingerboard and through the middle of the bridge.

# GÄRDEBY GÅNGLÅT

This is a "walking tune" (gånglåt) from the Swedish town of Gärdeby. It is played by fiddlers as they walk to a dance, or to the market.

Seascape    DON KERKHOF

# POLS
## NORWEGIAN FOLK DANCE

A pols is a dance in ¾ time from central Norway. I've heard this one played by several Wisconsin fiddlers. Unlike a waltz, where the accent is on the first beat alone, a pols has accents on the first and third beats.

Arr. © 1978 by R. Werner and D. Reiner. Used by permission.

# FINN JENTA WALTZ

This is a variant of a well-known Norwegian waltz, done in the style of Hans Brimi, a famous Norwegian folk fiddler. The title means "Finnish Girl". Occasionally, the F♯'s in the B part are played lower than normal, between F and F♯.

Arr. © 1978 by R. Werner. Used by permission.

58

# BLUES FIDDLING

From early African origins, to black field hollers, to country songsters in the late 1800's, to black jug bands in the 1920's—blues fiddling has roots which go a long way back. It is essentially music of the black, rural South.

When the first blues recordings became available in the early 1900's, Northern whites and blacks, particularly in Chicago, imitated the style, which is characterized by flatted 3rd and 7th notes in the scale, and a twelve-bar format. Many bluegrass, rock, and jazz fiddlers currently playing have been heavily influenced by the blues.

# BLUES FOR CINDY

Here's a twelve-bar blues tune with plenty of slides in it.

Play it smoothly ( ♪. ♫ ♪. ♫ can be relaxed to ♩ ₃ ♪♪ ♩ ₃ ♪. )
The straight eighth notes in measure nine are a nice contrast to the dotted
rhythms which come before them.

# BLUES IN A

This is a typical blues break, mainly improvised on the chords. The sixteenth notes in the first measure are grouped 6-6-4 instead of the usual 4-4-4-4, giving a nice syncopated effect. Note the fingering of the chromatic run at the beginning of measure two: 4-3-2-1 is easier than 3-2-2-1. In measures three and four, the rhythm slows repeatedly as you go from ♫♫♫♫ to ♫♫♫ to ♫♫ to ♩.

Chicken and Wheel    KATHRYN GERHARDT

# CAJUN FIDDLING

The French settlers of Acadia in eastern Canada were called "Acadiens". Because of harassment by the British, many of them migrated to Louisiana before the American Revolutionary War, where they remained fairly isolated from the rest of the population until the beginning of the twentieth century. There they came to be known as "Cajuns".

Cajun music, as it exists today, has been greatly affected by country-western and popular music, even though the traditional fiddle and Cajun **accordion** are still in almost every Cajun band.

# LA CASSINE SPECIAL

A lot of Cajun fiddlers tune their fiddles a full tone low ( ) so that they can play along with Cajun button accordions in the key of C. This gives the fiddle a hollow sound.

La Cassine Special should be played with slow slides and plenty of enthusiasm.

# Texas Style And Western Swing Fiddling

The combination of Southern rural traditions, Louisiana jazz, big band "swing", and Western cowboy life produced a style of music in the Southwest that is rather different from that of the old-timey string bands. Developed by men like Bob Wills, it is called Western Swing, and it depends heavily on fiddles, backed up by a driving, rhythmic beat.

In the same area of the country, notably in Texas, dance and contest fiddling have been polished to a fine art, resulting in a style of fiddling that is clean and precise. Many Texas style fiddlers are also expert at Western Swing, and often borrow its "swingy" feeling and improvisational techniques for their own playing.

# BEAUMONT RAG

Play this fine Texas-style tune with a bit of added swing, using [triplet figure] where [four notes] is written.

# DUSTY MILLER

Dusty Miller has a haunting feel to it, brought about by the consistently flatted seventh (G) in the A scale. Guitarists disagree on just how the tune should be chorded, possibly because fiddlers play so many slightly different versions.

Cacti    PAUL KAARAKKA

# SWING AND JAZZ FIDDLING

The violin has never been widely accepted as a jazz instrument, although musicians such as Stéphane Grappelli and Joe Venuti have been playing brilliantly since the 1920's. Certainly other styles of fiddling, such as bluegrass and Western Swing, have been affected by jazz.

Jazz or swing fiddlers are generally expert at improvisational playing, and are a good source of ideas for jazzing up your own fiddle playing.

# HARD CIDER

I would classify Hard Cider as a modern jazz tune. The rhythm is syncopated and the chord progression quite complex. At times, the notes in the improvised version seem to clash with the chords, making the overall effect very interesting. (Technically speaking, this is due to extensive chord substitution and frequent use of major seventh chords.) To make the tune swing, play ♩₃ ♪ or ♩. ♫ where ♫ is written. You will find harmony parts to the melody written out on page 84.

# SWANEE RIVER

Version I of Swanee River (spelled "Suwannee River" in Florida, where it is located) is fairly close to the melody until the end, but Version II really takes off. It is technically quite difficult, with syncopated rhythms and long sweeping runs of notes.

# CABLE

This is a true story about life's ups and downs, which originated in a high-rise apartment building in New Jersey. There is no chorus between the first two verses. The weaving countermelodies of the verse break work very well as a backup to the first verse, and flow right into the beginning of the second verse. The chorus break can serve as an instrumental lead or as backup for the chorus. As usual, play ♪₃♪ or ♩.♪ where ♪♪ is written to make the tune swing.

3. Well the elevator wouldn't budge,
   Although I gave it quite a nudge,
   Nearly broke my arm but brute force just **was not** enough.
   I didn't want to miss this date,
   And it was gettin' kinda late.
   Just 999 floors between me and my love. (Chorus)

4. I called the elevator man.
   He said, "I'm sorry, it's out of my hands.
   It worked when we bought it, you just caught it on a bad day."
   I kept on pressin' that button,
   But all my effort got me nothin'
   And when morning came this was all that I could say. (Chorus)

5. The next time that I saw Mabel,
   She was lookin' uncomfor - table.
   She said, "Where've you been, I been waitin' for your knock."
   I told her that I had tried,
   But she just up and sighed.
   She said, "Don't you know it gets lonely at the top." (Chorus)

Fiddle break for verse

Fiddle break for chorus

Mango Brothers Swing Band     MARY LUDINGTON

73

# IMPROVISATION

Within the old-timey tradition of fiddling, the melody must be fairly strictly adhered to, with only minor embellishments being permitted. At the other end of the spectrum, in jazz, swing, and to a lesser extent bluegrass, the melody is often merely the starting point for extensive development and modification by the fiddler. He may base his improvisation on the harmonic accompaniment (chords) of the tune, as well as the melody.

**Old-Timey:** Fiddlers may:
+ add drone strings to fill out chords;
+ anticipate certain key notes by playing them slightly before the beat;
+ change the octave in which the tune is played;
+ add occasional passing tones between the main melody notes;
+ make slight variations in the rhythm (e.g. 𝄞 instead of 𝄞 );
+ rock or shuffle the bow while a chord is held.

See Bile 'Em Cabbage Down as an example. Dance tunes and modal tunes are usually not modified at all.

**Bluegrass:** All of the techniques described above are used. In addition, the fiddler may:
+ choose tighter or bluesier chords than for old-timey playing;
+ use a sequence of chords to delineate a chord change

+ interpose many passing tones which flow constantly around the melody;
+ use complicated bowing and shuffle bowing patterns to accent the beat or offbeat;
+ play sequences of notes ("licks") which cross over bar lines.

See Soldier's Joy (Version III) and Blackberry Blossom as examples.

**Irish:** The best Irish fiddlers, while sticking quite close to the melody, manage to make each time through a tune sound a little bit different, by using a variety of turns and other embellishments. They may:
+ add a passing tone to change ♩ ♪ into 𝅘𝅥𝅮𝅘𝅥𝅮𝅘𝅥𝅮 or 𝅘𝅥𝅮𝅘𝅥𝅮, or to change 𝄞 into 𝄞 ;
+ use a very quick bow stroke triplet ( 𝄞 ) on a note;
+ shorten notes on the beat to imitate a piper ( 𝄞 instead of 𝄞 );
+ add one or more grace notes before a main melody note.

See the Kesh Jig and High Reel as examples.

**Scandinavian:** Turns and grace notes somewhat similar to those played by Irish fiddlers are often used. A very common technique is to:

+ reuse a note as an immediately following grace note (e.g.)

This grace note sometimes comes before the beat, sometimes on it. See the Finn Jenta Waltz and the Pols as examples.

**Blues:** Entire blues tunes or breaks are frequently improvised on the spot. Fiddlers who play blues tend to build up a repertoire of bluesy licks (e.g. the seventh measure of Blues for Cindy) which they piece together as they play. See Blues in A for an example of blues improvisation.

**Swing, Jazz, & Western Swing:** The fiddler usually plays the straight melody for the first time through, and after that the sky is the limit. He may:

+ delay a phrase and then catch up in a rush of notes;
+ anticipate a phrase by playing part of it before it is expected;
+ add long rippling sequences of passing tones;
+ vary the rhythm by using triplets or "swinging" dotted rhythms;
+ use double-stops (often done with a slight downward slide at the end) for their percussive effect;
+ shuffle the bow in complex patterns;
+ employ harmonics.

(Western Swing fiddlers will improvise much less, of course, if they are playing a traditional fiddle or dance tune.) See the Beaumont Rag, Swanee River, and Hard Cider as examples.

# TWIN (HARMONY) FIDDLING

Old-timey, Scandinavian, and Western Swing fiddlers often play in twos or threes, creating a rich texture of fiddle sound which is beautiful to listen to. Usually they play in parallel thirds, synchronizing their bowing. If you have never played in harmony with another fiddler, you're in for a treat.

# GOLDEN SLIPPERS

Golden Slippers is a good tune for square dances, and works perfectly for two fiddles.

# LIBERTY TWO-STEP

Liberty is another nice old-timey double fiddle tune. It works well in a medley with Mississippi Sawyer, since their A parts have the same chords. When the second fiddler is not playing exact harmony as is written here, he may play chords using the Nashville shuffle. This is known as "seconding", and is not so easy to do well.

78

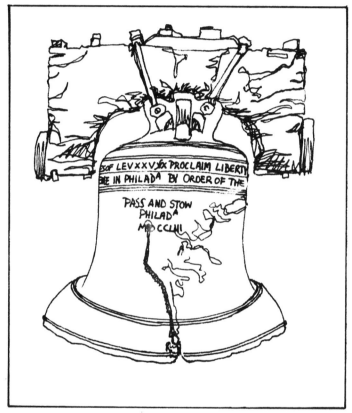

# GHOST

Ghost is a "jazzgrass" tune. It has been influenced by jazz, bluegrass, and even a little bit of classical music. Tunes of this type have been cropping up a lot lately, as bluegrass musicians seek to expand on traditional bluegrass. The second part may be played as counterpoint and harmony to the melody (Version I), or may acquire its own harmony and stand alone (Version II). Generally the bowings for the harmony parts follow those of the melody line.

81

# TYSKA POLSKA

This Swedish schottisch should be played with a lilting feel. Scandinavian fiddlers would probably syncopate the rhythm more than is written, playing measure one, for example, as

# INVITATION RAG

This rag is in the style of Western Swing. It begins with an arpeggiated climbing motif, and has a smooth and mellow B part.

# HARD CIDER

Here are the harmony parts to the melody of Hard Cider (see Swing and **Jazz** fiddling, page 69 ). Swing the tune by playing ♩₃♩ or ♩.♪ where ♪♪ is written. I've heard this triple version played on violin, saxophone, and trumpet, and it sounded rather eerie.

# DISCOGRAPHY

**Old-Timey**

| | |
|---|---|
| Old-Time Fiddle Classics | Country 507 |
| The Wonderful World of Old-Time Fiddlers | Vetco LP 104 |
| The Right Hand Fork of Rush's Creek (Wilson Douglas) | Rounder 0047 |
| Wild Rose of the Mountain (J.P. Fraley) | Rounder 0037 |
| Parkersburg Landing (Ed Haley) | Rounder 1010 |
| Clark Kessinger, Fiddler | Folkways FA 2336 |
| Learn to Fiddle Country Style (Tracy Schwarz) | Folkways FI 8359 |
| The Fuzzy Mountain String Band | Rounder 0010 |
| The Hollow Rock String Band | Rounder 0024 |

**Bluegrass**

| | |
|---|---|
| A Baker's Dozen (Kenny Baker) | Country 730 |
| Dad's Favorites (Byron Berline) | Rounder 0100 |
| The Bluegrass Session (Vassar Clements) | Flying Fish FF 038 |
| Curly Ray Cline | Rebel SLP-1566 |
| The Greatest Hits of Benny Martin | Gusto Records PO #223 |
| Chubby Fiddles Around (Chubby Wise) | Stoneway STY 105 |

**Irish**

| | |
|---|---|
| The Wheels of the World | Shanachie Records 33001 |
| The Boys of the Lough (any album) | Philo Records |
| The Chieftains (any album) | e.g., Island Records ILPS 9364 |
| Andy McGann & Paddy Reynolds | Shanachie Records 29004 |

**Scandinavian**

| | |
|---|---|
| Folk Fiddling from Sweden | Nonesuch H-72033 |
| The American-Swedish Spelmans Trio | Rounder 6004 |
| Glamos Spelemannslag (Norwegian) | RCA FLPS 6 |

**Blues**

| | |
|---|---|
| Martin, Bogan, and Armstrong | Flying Fish 003 |

**Cajun**

| | |
|---|---|
| The Balfa Brothers Play Traditional Cajun Music | Swallow LP-6011 |
| The Cajun Country Fiddle of Rufus Thibodeaux | La Louisianne LL 129 |

**Texas**

| | |
|---|---|
| Texas Fiddle Favorites | County 707 |
| Texas Dance Party (Johnny Gimble) | Columbia KC 34284 |
| Country Fiddling from the Big State (Benny Thomasson) | County 724 |

**Western Swing**

| | |
|---|---|
| Western Swing, Historic Recordings | Old-Timey LP 105 |
| Hall of Fame (Bob Wills & Tommy Duncan) | United Artists UAS 9962 |
| Spade Cooley | Club of Spade #00103 |

**Swing and Jazz**

| | |
|---|---|
| I Got Rhythm (Stephane Grappelli) | Black Lion Records BL-047 |
| Django '35-'39 (Stephane Grappelli) | GNP Crescendo Records GNP 9019 |
| Stuff Smith | Everest FS-238 |
| Joe Venuti & George Barnes | Concord Jazz CJ-30 |

Open Mike Session at Pickin' and Grinnin'
Workshop in the Wisconsin Dells     HUGH DEVANEY

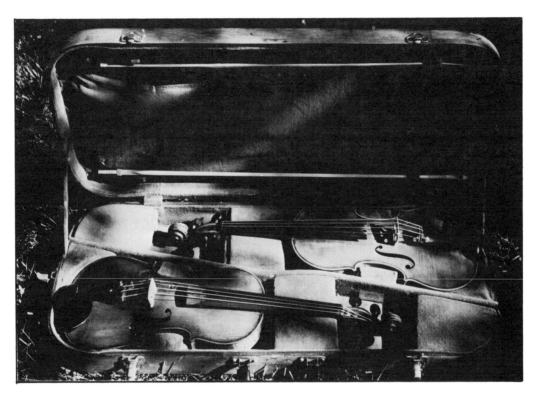

Twin Fiddles     PAUL KAARAKKA